Calculator
RIDDLES

ISBN 0-439-22671-6

12 11 10 9 8 7 6 5 4 3 2 1   0 1 2 3 4 5/0

Printed in the U.S.A.   23

First Scholastic revised edition printing, September 2000

Calculator
RIDDLES

David A. Adler
illustrated by
Cynthia Fisher

SCHOLASTIC INC.

New York Toronto London Auckland Sydney
Mexico City New Delhi Hong Kong

A calculator is a whiz at doing math problems. Most calculators can also be used to write words. That's because eight of the digits when looked at upside down are letters.

Turn on your calculator. (Some calculators use a solar cell and don't need to be turned on.) There should be an O. in the display window. If not, press the C key.

Look at the other keys. All calculators have one key for each digit: 1, 2, 3, 4, 5, 6, 7, 8, 9, and 0. There are also keys marked •, =, +, −, ×, and ÷.

Now take a look at the digits upside down. Many of them look like letters. Press the 8 key. Turn your calculator around. The 8 is now a B. Upside down 3 becomes E. The number 9 becomes G; 4 becomes h; 1 becomes I; 7 becomes L; 0 becomes O; 5 becomes S.

Enter 14 on your calculator. Turn your calculator around. Can you read "Hi"?

Now enter 4509 and then turn your calculator around again. Can you read "GOSH"?

With only eight letters and only eight spaces on most calculators, there are a limited number of words that can be written. But still, you can have lots of fun. You can find the answers to calculator riddles.

First, read the riddles in this book. Then, with your calculator, solve the math problem that follows each riddle. Turn your calculator upside down. The digits will spell a word or words, the answer to the riddle. Of course, since on a calculator there can be no blank spaces, answers of more than one word will run together.

If you have trouble finding the answers to the riddles, turn to page 32.

Have fun!

1. What did Santa say in his garden?

Answer: 190 × 100 + 19 × 16 =

2. Hello! **Hello!**
You still can't hear?
What will make an ear hear?

Answer: 28 × 8 ÷ 56 =

3. If little William ate ice cream, pickles, candy, and sardines, little William would become . . .

Answer:
$77 \times 100 + 19 \times 1,000 - 229 =$

4. What's the best answer to someone who calls you a turkey?

Answer: $1000 - 53 \times 400 + 9 =$

5. What did Jack
   say to Jill
   after she
   tumbled down
   the hill?

Answer: $257 \times 2 \times 50 + 57 \times 2 =$

6. What was Little Bo Beep's middle name?

Answer: $10 \times 10 \div 125 =$

7. Humpty Dumpty had a great fall. Out flowed the white. Out came the yellow. And what part of Mr. Dumpty could not be repaired?

Answer: $773 \times 20 + 9 \times 50 + 9 \times 100 + 93 =$

8. It honks but isn't a car.
It flies but isn't a jet.
It floats but isn't a boat.
What is it?

Answer:

$50 \times 7 \times 100 + 9 =$

9. It's strange. These come in many different sizes but they are always exactly one foot long.

Answer: $53 \times 40 \times 5 + 9 \times 5 =$

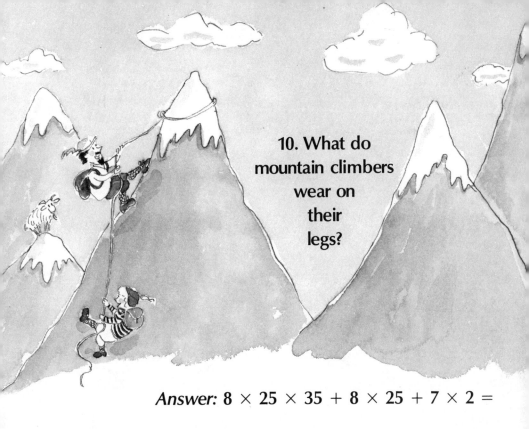

10. What do mountain climbers wear on their legs?

Answer: $8 \times 25 \times 35 + 8 \times 25 + 7 \times 2 =$

11. What comes in the middle of every August but in no other month?

Answer: $1323 \div 7 \div 21 =$

12. If 33 is lots and 66 is lots more, what is 21?

Answer: $20 \times 55 \times 5 + 37 =$

13. What happens after a rude dinner guest has soup, salad, hamburger, and pie, and there's nothing left to eat?

Answer:
$20 \times 25 + 31 \times 4 \times 125 - 33 \times 2 =$

14. What do you put into every pair of pants you wear, and every pair of jeans?

Answer: 821 + 2417 + 1498 + 1201 =

15. What does every married couple hope to always have?

Answer: 613 × 45 + 4 × 2 =

16. George Washington didn't need a bed because he wouldn't . . .

Answer: $35 \times 9 + 2 =$

17. Who invented the telephone but had no one to call?

Answer: $193 \times 20 + 9 \times 2 =$

18. What are long, thin, and wet and discovered electricity before Benjamin Franklin?

Answer: $8 \times 80 - 3 \times 9 =$

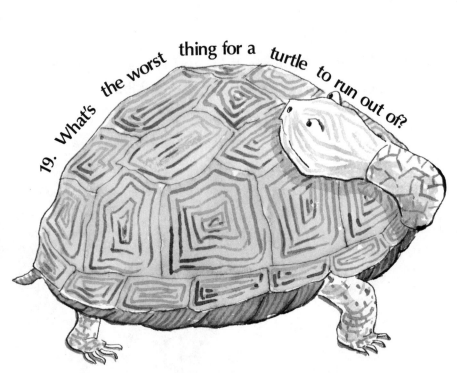

19. What's the worst thing for a turtle to run out of?

Answer: **200 × 75 + 469 × 50 × 100 + 514 =**

20. What has just three letters but is not small?

Answer: **561 ÷ 11 × 18 =**

21. The fisherman used a lightning rod and hoped to catch an . . .

Answer: $10 \times 10 \times 10 - 267 =$

22. What would you call someone who keeps telling you what to do?

Answer: $20 \times 70 - 23 \times 4 =$

23. What do babies say when they're picked up?

Answer: $9 \times 1001 \div 10 \div 100 \div 100 =$

24. What are made of ICE

to keep people WARM?

Answer: $50 \times 40 \times 250 + 791 =$

25. What's the nicest thing you can get a bear who's caught in a trap?

Answer: 50 × 700 + 7 =

26. What can change an ear into a bear?

Answer: $109 \times 48 \div 6 \div 109 =$

27. What would you
call someone sitting
in a bowl of
ice cream?

Answer: 16 × 20 + 3 × 25 =

28. What do little laughing hyenas do?

Answer: 200 × 19 × 100 − 81 =

29. The runner was fast. He beat hundreds of others in the race. Then he said, "I can't race again. I'm so tired now, I couldn't even beat . . .

Answer: $12 \times 50 - 1 \times 10 + 3 =$

30. What do cute little piglets become?

Answer: $50 - 9 \times 5 \times 16 \times 100 + 51 \times 18 =$

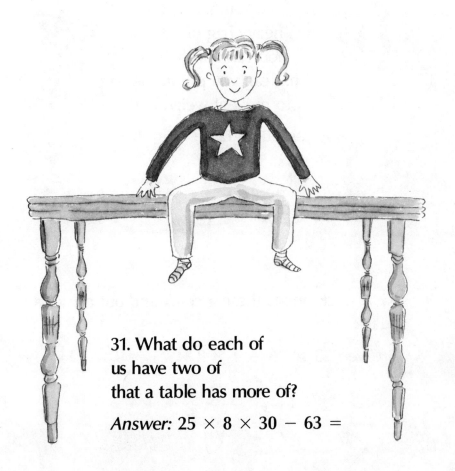

31. What do each of
us have two of
that a table has more of?

Answer: $25 \times 8 \times 30 - 63 =$

**32. You have a big,
heavy bag of beans.
You can hardly lift it.
What can you put in the bag
to make it weigh less?**

Answer: $20 \times 125 \div 5 - 37 \times 8 =$

33. A duck opens these a crack and out comes a quack.

Answer: $23 \times 25 + 2 \times 2 \times 25 + 9 \times 2 =$

34. What kind of guns do yellow jackets shoot?

Answer: $100 \times 89 \times 100 - 277 \times 6 =$

**35. You don't need a pot.
You don't need a flame.
This is all you need to
make oil boil.**

Answer: $129 \times 40 \div 645 =$

36. I have eyes,
a tongue,
and sometimes
a foot.
What am I?

Answer: $25 \times 8 + 3 \times 15 =$

THE WORLD

37. Give me a spin. I'm the world
we're in. What am I?

Answer:
$47 \times 8 \div 4 \times 5 \times 9 + 1 \times 9 =$

38. I
chase
and
chase your toes
but I never catch them.
What am I?

Answer: $61 \times 60 + 7 \times 2 =$

39. I can be big.
I can be small.
But big or small
I weigh nothing
at all.
What am I?

Answer: $20 \times 25 - 37 \times 8 =$

40. When ghosts chew gum, what do they blow?

Answer:

$170 \times 20 - 39 \times 200 + 51 \times 8 =$

41. What do little ghosts get when they fall down the stairs?

Answer:

$939 \div 3 \times 16 \times 10 \times 100 + 8 =$

42. When friendly ghosts meet they smile, shake hands and say, "How do you . . .

Answer: $10 \div 125 =$

43. In a restaurant, first comes the hamburger, then the fries and soda. And next comes the . . .

Answer: $100 \times 10 \div 4 \times 16 - 141 \times 2 =$

44. What was the Big Bad Wolf's first name?

Answer:
$36 + 14 \times 9 + 9 \times 2 =$

45. What's in your bathroom and in your chair
and even after your bath it's still in your hair?

Answer: 98 × 4 ÷ 98 =

ANSWERS

1. 304304, HOEHOE
2. 4, H
3. 7718771, ILLBILL
4. 378809, GOBBLE
5. 51514, HISIS
6. 0.8, BO
7. 77345993, EGGSHELL
8. 35009, GOOSE
9. 53045, SHOES
10. 350414, HIHOSE
11. 9, G
12. 5537, LESS
13. 530934, HEGOES
14. 5937, LEGS
15. 55178, BLISS
16. 317, LIE
17. 7738, BELL
18. 5733, EELS
19. 77345514, HISSHELL
20. 918, BIG
21. 733, EEL
22. 5508, BOSS
23. 0.09009, GOOGOO
24. 500791, IGLOOS
25. 35007, LOOSE
26. 8, B
27. 8075, SLOB
28. 379919, GIGGLE
29. 5993, EGGS
30. 5904918, BIGHOGS
31. 5937, LEGS
32. 3704, HOLE
33. 57718, BILLS
34. 5338338, BEEBEES
35. 8, B
36. 3045, SHOE
37. 38079, GLOBE
38. 7334, HEEL
39. 3704, HOLE
40. 5378008, BOOBLES
41. 5008008, BOOBOOS
42. 0.08, BOO
43. 7718, BILL
44. 918, BIG
45. 4, H